A Silent Noisy Walk in my Mind

A Silent Noisy Walk in my Mind

An Anthology of Poems

Kwasi Ntem-Mensah

Published by Tablo

Table of Contents

Thank You

CREDIT: Book cover design by Tony S Habada

PERSEVERANCE

Each day we make an effort at something. We seek to accomplish something. We set a goal or goals. We know not how we will do it but we aim to do it. There are obstacles in our way. A million of them but we aim to forge ahead. Do you prepare before embarking on a project? How long does it take you to prepare? Do you rush through your preparations or do you take your time? Are you patient? Do you think about how you will accomplish it?

There are many that you can name that did not end being who they were/are overnight. It took and takes hard work to get there. They knew it will be hard. I am telling you, it will be hard but in your heart, do it. Persevere.

If you plan and really plan well, then you will have confidence in yourself. That is Very important.

If you are walking or running, you could slip and fall. Don't stay down; get up because in your heart you know must get there. You will get there. That is Determination of Purpose.

Move on. The road is not smooth. It is muddy and rough. Persevere. You will get there. You know you will. Heaven is your guide. Only You can - knm

" His works has made a significant difference in my life. It's remarkable, riveting — but I'd always like to see more!"- Nada Sika N

"I started reading to patronize a friend but I left with more. I learned how to appreciate his words and it has increased my personal growth further." Terry K

'Not only is his works both fun and challenging but an 'attitudinal thinking' becomes a way of thought." George "Ras" P

Acknowledgments

GRATEFUL TO GOD ALMIGHTY, HE HATH BROUGHT ME THIS FAR.

KW and VV, my beloved parents, you live on.
Trudy, Nana Kwame, V.V. and Portia, love you to bits
Yaw, Kwabena, Afua- siblings supreme
Tony Turbo, I am very grateful.
Ishmael, Eric, RABS, and the silent noisemakers out there, I wish you:
Above all good health,
In tandem with long life,
All others will flow.
For it is,
Blessings Always!

My prayer

On bend knees I,
Ask for help, Creator mine
Next minute unknown,
I run rough and dirty,
Amends to make only mine,
On bend knees I
Give thanks, for your grace
Still thanks I give,
For that called LIFE
With its generator of breath
Grateful I am for a heartbeat.
I sprawl before thee in Thanksgiving
#SILENTNOISES

In The begining ...

In the beginning
You smiled at everything and everyone
For no reason.
You just smiled.
In the beginning
You worked liked a John Bull
For no reason.
You just upped and worked.
In the beginning
You were tolerant.
For no reason.
All the ridicule and the gossip and belittling
For no reason.
You endured it all.
In the beginning
You swallowed your pride.
They trampled upon you.
Today, you made it not.
It was outside.
The upheavals, the shallow breathing
You are fed up.
Something ought to be done.
You spoke your heart.
You are human.
Loving, caring, humble, compassionate, passionate.
In the ending
The bile is out

Before

Finally, I am going to meet my person that is if no one interrupts
my sleep. I see the look on your face. You doubt me, right? I
know what you are thinking. No, I am not deranged. The people
you think are my people are not my people. These people I do
not know and I regret knowing.

Let us go meet my people. They are the royals of Anomabo.
Their last name is Duker. We are a wonderful people. We are
very hospitable and loving. Nothing about us depicts us as royals
because we exhibit simplicity in character and behavior. My
great-grandfather is the middle -aged man you met on your way
coming in. He is the chief of Anomabo. Those four young men
seated on the benches are his sons; Kwasi Panyin and Kwasi
Kakra, Yaw and Kwabena. Kwasi Panyin is my grandfather and
father of my father who has not been born yet. Do not be
surprised; I will explain all this to you.

Let me first describe the palace to you. It is painted white and
has a beautiful artistically designed wooden gate. There is an
artist's impression of a lion with a scorpion as its tail boldly
painted on the gate. It virtually covers the gate. This gate leads
into a courtyard that is more like a fruit garden; nothing like you
have ever seen. I leave you to imagine the fruits herein; tropical
fruits. This is where my grandfather and his brothers engaged in
their nocturnal ventures.(Do not go over thinking-simply means
where they hung out with the ladies of their dreams before
marriage. Nothing untoward took place because it is a taboo to
do it in a farm or farm-like place and every man wants to marry
a virgin. Do not forget to be a virgin brought so much respect to
both parents and future husband and in-laws.) The low hanging
leafy tree branches create a cozy environment but the floor is
packed earth. When it rains, nobody wants to walk around or go
there. The stairs leading to the stately welcome room is about

the length of two football fields. It is only 7 stairs high. Beyond that are doors wide enough to fit seven elephants through side by side. The intricate carvings on the wooden doors are unimaginable. The room in itself, though sparsely furnished, is elegant in appearance and splendor.

This is my first time meeting my people, so I want to be sure I make no mistake lest they deny me. They are in a crisis meeting. It is a rather serious issue. This issue had occurred during the period of the great rainfall; when houses had been washed away together with all its occupants. Actually that was about six years ago.

Back to the issue at hand. Men outnumbered the women. The number of women who were ripe for marriage and motherhood had diminished. It was possible some of the men would have no women to warm their beds or prepare sumptuous dishes to assuage their hungers on coming home from the farms. When this issue had last taken place, it was men that was in short supply. The whole place is suddenly noisy with silence. Heads turn almost three hundred and sixty degrees. I forgot. My men's eternity cologne stands out like a rainbow.

My great-grandfather the chief, beckons in a low but assuring booming voice "welcome home son, welcome. Look how big you have grown. Where is everybody? Mama Vida,boys, all of you come here. Kwasi has come home. Now is it a short visit? How long will you be here?" I never was able to answer for then I heard another voice screaming, "you have been sleeping for too long. I thought the afternoons were for naps not sleep"

If only

If only,
I could see through your eyes
If only,
I could use your hands
If only
I could walk with your feet
If only,
I could chew with your teeth
If only,
I could hear with your ears
If only,
I could express myself using your feelings and emotions
If only,
I could allow you to be me for a minute, for an hour, for a day
If only,
Only then would you understand my joy and my pain.

Elections

Elections
Donkomi Donkomi
Buy me
Buy my vote
Yes Yes Yes
I am for sale
I am without fate
You can never fail
Donkomi. Donkomi
Sell me
To your people
I need your vote
Yes Yes Yes
Sell me
I am the best
The biggest and better liar
I am ready to steal your money
I am ready at the starter's gun to be
CORRUPT

Corrupted Innocence

Where once stood justice
greed and avarice are rooted.
Pillars of salt
Can and will be washed
Erection that will bear fruit
Must stand
Love, Peace, Truth, Justice,
Rooted by perseverance with sisterly determination
Sweet innocence
Will smile
Again

Understand Me

I want I want I want
That is all I want
A word with my father
A chance to prepare me
I want my Father
I want I want I want
If only for a minute
To lay my head on my mother
A chance to cuddle me
I want my mother
I would give anything to hear your thunder
Softened by mama's melodious note
Nothing would put us asunder
I would never talk by rote
These days are tough, I have never seen
These times, as they crawl rushing,
December is now January
12 begets 1 in a flash.
I want to wash my brain
Hang them out to dry, on a drying line
Two pegs to hold, at the end and end
Who will unzip my head so I can send?
The brain is deep shafted mine
Yet shallow like a bird's water bowl.
Give me detergent to wash the filth
To do away with the grime
Can you believe all is slime?
O my brain, await my gentle sway
The scrubbing brushes will not make way
Like a strait jacket

Lowered into the pits of darkness
Struggling to burst forth yet stymied.
Lay still still still
Call on HIM
To freedom and light
Yes Father yes mother
It is great chatting again!

Dum Di Dum

Dum di dum dum di dum
Yellow or black
White or Caucasian
Negro, Asian, Aryan
The river is red
That course through
Us
Same organs
Functioning in
Us
I give a name
Stool name
You give a number
Roman numerals
Contempt is your middle name
Hospitality
That is my name
Acceptance is the key
We are all one
From the
Creator
Bless us all

Her Ode

One is many
Truth be told
You are open
Yet very firm
Humor is your game
It is thine fame
Yaa Asantewaa is gone
She lives
You wonder
Yet you are bold
For you are gold
Many start
Yet love the pecunia
You are peculiar
In that you are true
The blood is pure

Write

WRITE

You write
I write
We write
She writes
He writes
They claim right
We are right

It is part of us
We write
In dreams, In walks
We write
Lifting you up
We scatter the truth

8 letters

8 letters
Of inequality
That is EQUALITY
Put me down
Raise another
Same stock
Color same
Ancestors same
Red in veins
10 letters make up INEQUALITY
TREAT ME
As my brother
Sister,sister. Sister
Hold my hand I pray
We are stuck in clay
Crack the pot
Loosen the grip
Be equal
Experience

One People

Black
White
Yellow

Asian
European
African

Wide nose
Aquiline nose
Slanted eyes
Desert
Jungle Sea

Red blood
One people
One race

What?

INFORMATION
What you do not know
MISINFORMATION
What they want you to know
NEWS
What you are made to know
JOURNALISM
Study of lies
TRUTH
Well told lie
FACT
What is hidden

Authority

Permit me to laugh
Do you expect me to cry?
I laugh at your ignorance
Your authority should be a
Guide to your leadership role
Not pontificating

Out of respect
I sought permission to laugh
In reality I laugh
Ask for help
You are lost
You need it

Authority
Does not make you a god
Back to HUMILITY
Three words
Discerning, Discretion, Timeliness

Large as Small

Can you see me?
I am the large giant
The one standing not behind you
You surprise me
Why can't you see me?
My size allows me to stand out
I am the thick tall bug
With the ROAR of an ant
My footsteps cause the seas to vibrate
Dare me and I will swallow you whole
It will take an eternity
I believe in myself
My Supreme does too
Lack of belief
You will perish
Obstacles you put
Obstacles I surmount

Dance

I will dance to the beat
I do not have a choice
Dance-able or not dance-able
I am on the floor
The master drummer knows
Not his craft
This is not a dance
This is hopscotch.

I will dance to the beat
I have a choice
This is dance-able
The master drummer is new
Old master knew
He could not drum a beat
The new beat is of Hope,
The new rhythm is Love and Unity
The new chorus is Understanding

He assures and reassures
We are all dancing
We are all enjoying
The drums thunder relentlessly

Veggies

When I was a child
I did not like veggies
Today I am married
I love my wife and kids
I want to be a role model
I want to be a loving husband
I still do not like veggies
I eat them to set an example

Learning

Learning, learning, learning, learning
Ever so expanding knowledge
One or more to benefit
Only to be buried one day

Real Dragons

As we sat in our homes
Calabash in hand, kola in the other
Asking the Supreme Being,
Sharing with our brothers
We knew Him but in our way
We sat in our homes
And you came in big boats
With rooms down and up
Dark and stinking
With crosses all over
We came out of our homes
Arms wide and inviting
Bible in hand, gun in the other
Sugar in your mouth, pepper under your tongue
Dragons are never mystical
There is a fire in your breath
We were shackled as you burned our homes
Telling us the devil is in us
You had the guns and the evil mind
You put us on your boats
You on top, we were under
Our new home was dark and humid
Rats for neighbors day and night
Fighting us over what is food
Day is night and night is day
Time is lost
Yet we believe in our GOD
Descendants discern
We realize you lied
And yet still lie

Oppression is the norm, through mental slavery
By any means necessary
Claiming it be of your God
Such hypocrisy, such idiocy
A New You

Bear no grudge

Bear no grudge
do not say
"I will not budge"
challenge you I may
or very possibly to wedge
causing a shift in where you lay
never say nay
for then its quicksand
you are stuck
dare to take a plunge
when you come up
for air
"A new you" will
emerge
shining to the world
all because of you
moved from the edge.

Confused

Confused
Round and Square we go
confused and misinterpreting
the message is clear
discerning the truth
A lie can be true
only 'cos it is the truth of a lie
which makes it a fact
for then, it is the truth of a lie
spewed forth

Chapter 1 Who is he ?

"I am told just like you have been told through stories that were
told to us by the griots ... stop. We have no griots in Ghana; we
have praise singers. They will sing your idiotic praises for a few
pesewas just to water down the drought in their throat. There is
desertification taking place in the esophagus of a human
mammal. I digress.

What were you told? You have forgotten so soon? How long ago?
Since when did you stop suckling on your mother's breasts?
Almost twenty years ago? You are older now I presume. You are
old in age yet young in the grey matter. You have refused
to........... And still do behave and process thoughts as a baby.
You are in awe because I dare speak my mind.

It is true we are told to be respectful of our elders but if the truth
is hidden in the tunnel that every human longs to come through
to applause but these days we are removed... I digress again. You
know that red tunnel, right? If the truth were hidden in it and
you use all means either genuine or dubious to remove it
especially if it is your mother's, have you committed incest?
Have ever thought about the people who think about you? The
red river meanders through them just like you. The same
mountains and valleys, ponds and tributaries. I forget you have
had alterations done to your self that these people cannot afford
to. When sick they go back to the Creator who molded them to
heal them........................"

My grandfather is my great grandfather's head of army. The
townsfolk revere him. I am meeting him just like you for the first
time but I cannot believe how humble he is. He does not allow
the praises to get to his head. Though not lettered much, he is

able to keep accurate records of events. He is addressing one of the town chiefs for looking down upon the people whom he is supposed to serve. Why do you keep interrupting when I am trying to explain things to you? Yes to answer your question; he is that short man standing there. The stout short man, charcoal black in complexion with a full face of jet-black hair. See how they hail him especially the ladies? He is bold, fearless yet very loving. We never could hear to the end his speech because we have to go wait for him in his house else we might miss him. I am hoping to have a one on one meeting with him. I am hoping to receive his blessings. I am hoping to eat lunch with him. I am hoping to have him all to myself even if for a second. He is my grandfather. We have the same name. I am he.

Patience
I saw patience
Suitors walked, crawled, run
Patience
Soft spoken
Loved me on eggshells
3 sons 2 daughters
Patience
Arm in mine
Eternally locked
Proud out and in
Still young at heart
In the beginning to the beginning

Whole

Sentiments, Emotions, Empathy
Feeling, Love
Lust, Wish, Admire, Imagine
You are wondering
Do not ponder
Beyond the border
For that is the order
I am the other
Piece
Fulfilling the WHOLE

Glass

Glass
What glass
Drinking glass
What color
What shape
What size
What are the contents
What is the state
What is the length
What is the width
What is the circumference
What is the diameter
What type of glass
Who are you?

Thinking

1 plus 1 is 2
2 plus 2 is 4
so they say
so society has bought
it has become the norm
to accept without ......
What is one?
What are the two?
Who made it so?
Could 1 have been named different?
Would you have accepted
The box
In the Box
The round Box?
Are you out or in?
In is out and out is in

Are you thinking?

Beauty

I perpetually gaze into your eyes
I am enchanted
I am whole
I have peace
I am peace
You have given me peace

Drawn into this beauty
Beauty pure and golden
Beauty was seen by me
Beauty experienced by all
Beauty that glows like a
DIAMOND

A rare gem of a diamond
I am at peace
A whole new creation
Your patience and love
Your words of comfort
Of inspiration, of encouragement

Beauty is from within
Like a plant, it germinates
It permeates the outer
The creamy white, chocolate
Ebony black complexions
Will numb your senses
The real beauty lies
Underneath
The real beauty
I will always cherish

I adore You

???

Libation is poured to the Supreme One
Acknowledgment
He was, is, will be
Born on a Saturday
Otwedeampong Kwame
Created all
The earth is His
Born on a Thursday
Asaase Yaa
Beliefs so entrenched
Held dear
Guiding principles
Molded way of life
There was reverence
Cultured way of life
Respect, Honesty, Integrity,
Divine was sacred
Exalted
Oracles
Consulted, foretold
With precision
Events to unfold
Societal vices shunned

A dark man was
Commissioned
By Nana Nyame
He wrote a book
Long before
In a language unknown
Letters unknown

Stolen, adulterated.
Words changed. Promotion of Mastery
But some words hold true
The book still is
Divinely inspired it
Was
Put on a vessel
Brought to a person
Amassed on a land
Named after a Roman
Africanus
Nubia is her name
Kush for the gems
Sought to tell us
The devil spawned us
What a lie
Told us God lives in a
Book
What a lie
He has only one son
What a lie
That only their religion is true
What a lie
Now everybody lies
There is no fear
Respect has gone to the dogs
Cheating and chanting
In the name of Jesus
The thief equally
Seeking protection
In their endeavors

Dare you to do that
In a traditional way

Words hurt and have come
To demean
A shrine is seen as evil
Connotes evil; of the devil
The book as written defines marriage
It defines households
It defines sacrifices
Today, you scream for money
In lieu of sacrifices
You have taught our people
How to fleece their own
Wealth is Christianity
Christianity is riches
Riches is a status quo
Knowledge is good
Write our own; tell our own
None can say our story
They never saw it happen.

My Story

My story can only be told by my Creator
My story is my experience
My story is me
My story is my story
I do not need your applause
I do not need your sympathy
I do not need your comfort
I speak from my heart
I hunt and fish in my mind
My story, our story, your story
I am only a messenger
I have come to deliver.

A walk in my mind

I am wandering
Along stony paths
Along winding rivers
It only sends shivers
I need no sympathy
Though you are wondering
Why I walk in my mind
I only seek what is sought
It is only in my thought
because I have to think
through the well of the ink
I hope it does not run dry
because then I would cry
I want answers
Yet they elude me in the fog
Or do I need a guide dog
Education is good enough
It is deemed a road rough
But it has always served
Though few have swerved
Answers in the grave
Gone forever

In God we trust

I pray for her
You prey on her
You are bold to defend your cause of looting
I am bold to defend the cause of freedom
You take away my rights
In gentle tones, you convince me to oppress myself
The ramblings and rants of a cash crazed elite
Who dwells on the dollar frequency to trod
Ever so sure confuse me
You prey on her
I pray for her
In the pulpit, you stand
Calling for a tenth though I do not work
Tell that to the vultures
I forget you are one
Cloaked in a book written by my forebears
Stolen and given to you by my would-be oppressors
You prey on me. Vulture!
I pray for Her so you stop preying on Her
I pray for true humility for you
I pray for you to cherish, uphold
Honesty with Absolute Fearlessness
I pray for you to rise up and resist
Smooth tongues are persuasive

Weep not

Mummy Africa, weep not
Pardon us for we have failed,
Greed and avarice
Topped with selfishness,
Has become our lot
We, your newborns
Pledge unconditionally
No matter where we are
To put a smile on your face.
Unity of purpose topped
With selflessness
Is our forte
God bless Africa.

1:00 a.m.

We sit at the river banks
In no order of ranks
Mothers laid bare
As sons stare
Fathers equally stark
While daughters gaze
The shame is gone
It is about survival
You oppressed
Today you are still oppressing
You have no shame
Though you claim sorry
Yet you do not worry
For that is your fame
To quench the flame
Impossible
'Cos we will rise again
Melanin and pituitary gland
Is our claim
You tried to destroy
Truth never dies
Like a stream sunken
One day it will up
Feed the thirsty
Who yearn to learn
We are who we are
Humble in spirit yet resilient
I am only a messenger
I have come to deliver

One life to live

.... And when I am departed
Do not say
Neither do cry
Nor wail
Yet still
To mourn and broadcasting
He / She is my friend; I loved him / her so
For you despised me
Plotted to cause my downfall
Put me in darkness
Even refused to admit I was a living being
I am departed
From you. For good.
But wait.
I am certainly alive.
I never died.

Always

                    To the Highest
We can never be that high
Only by His grace
For it is not a race
He hath brought us far
On a musical note, fa
So we shall dance
For we are eager
Like the tiger
Never the dunce

The Chair

Sit.
Sit The Chair.
Sit On The Chair.
Please, sit on The Chair
Tones
Ringing tones
Speech tones
Dialog tones
Make the mood
I see a chair
The Chair
I cannot sit
I have to be asked
Not told
The Chair
Many contenders
Do not be pretenders
Precise Hypocrites
Swayed with crates
The Chair
Is not for the Hare
Neither the Mare
It is for the Rare
Who has us at Heart.
Please, sit on the Chair!

Behalf

On my behalf
On their behalf
On our behalf
Whose behalf
Who is clever by half
Are you a calf
Unless you are not whole
And yes you are truly half
Come with me
Did you leave half
Mind and body?
Go. Leave.
Did you leave half
So why behalf
It begs my mind
Like celebrating birthdays
Not our birth dates
Dare you ask
It begins with you
On your own behalf

Thinking

We are thinking
About what
Though there is an inkling
In part
Though it is whole
We are confused
'Cos we have refused
To admit
To remit
Our brains
Better things
We dwell
In the well
Of constant
Greed and self- aggrandizement
Built as a monument
Palatial edifice
White elephant
In our minds
You think I think we are thinking
None have that calling
'Except we call on The Most High
Not they who are up high
Stop thinking
Be guided
Do good

Mothers

Our mothers
Long term
Short term
Regular term
Still our mothers
Our mothers
Formula-fed
Breastfed
Spoon fed
Hand-fed
Still our mothers
Teachers, Lawyers,
Doctors, Prostitutes,
Nurses, Kayay3,
Judges, Drivers,
Soldiers, House helps
Still our mothers
In labor, the pain
To watch, in pain
a child in pain
Only to call
Names without pain
Our mothers, who are
Still our mothers
Sick or healthy
Departed or Alive
Thank you is all we have
'Cos, yes, and God bless you always
You are still our Mothers

Here

Here but not here
Seeing but blind
Speaking yet dumb
Writing but scratching
Understanding yet wondering
How we shall depart
We know not
For even the seeing are blind
Deaf and dumb
Speak and hear better
Live the life
That God be praised
Blessings Always

What is man?

What is Man?
What is Selflessness?
What is Self-glorification?
What is Humility?
What is Self-worship?
What is Arrogance?
Why do some people seek glorification for every little thing they do for others or acknowledgment for everything?
Are those people truly happy?
Does self-importance make for happiness?
Or it brings a limited level of satisfaction? Does it last though?
Is it Satisfaction we seek in life or Happiness?
What makes for Happiness?
Is Happiness the same as Satisfaction?
Who are you?
Who am I?
Are all people equal?
Does Money or Education and/or both make a person better than others?
Who is to say what a man would be in the future?
Does any man hold the key to any other man's future?
If you can help a person get ahead in life, how many such people did you help?
Or did selfishness, greed, and envy get in the way?
How many people would help someone get ahead of him?
If you claim you are kindhearted, when was the last time you gave a little money to someone who you know needs it?
Ask yourself what your family thinks of you? No, not your wife/ husband or kids, but your extended family?
Then ask your wife/husband to be honest with you.
Do you go to church? Why?

Is it for fashion, gossip, laugh at others? Why do you go to church?

Do you think you can tell me what the pastor said?

What is church all about? Do you make time for God in the hamlet of your home?

If not, does 2 hrs in the church make up for that?

Are we truly Selfless and Loving?

Who are we?

What is Man?

What is our purpose here?

Are we here just to procreate, selfless and Loving to our family, yet closed and uncaring to the world around us? And just pass through life?

Show me an unselfish man?

Take what you lack within and make thyself better before God and Man.

The Rainbow

When ugly knocks at your door
You open and say with vim
"Hello Beautiful.."
Speak the truth
Say 'Ugly'
Are you hurt?
Are you dead?
Why do you fear the truth?
Say it as it is.
You are a hypocrite.
Yes, I do not love you
Your smiles are serpentine
Your fangs ready to pierce
Why do you fear the truth
I am ashamed
To call you my friend
You hate the truth
Call ugly ugly
I have seen light-skinned
I have seen multi-colored rainbows
I have seen black turned yellow
I have laughed
I will laugh
I am laughing.
Dedicated to RABS; they love the truth

TAMA Lady- an African beauty

I love my coffee
Sweet like your toffee
That is your candy
But my dandy
Sweet black and strong
On two powerful absorbents
Two stereo speakers
The apex of a Bluetooth
I have a sweet tooth
Cooks with love
Dainty as a dove
Slender flexible.smooth arms
A rare African gem
Piercing deep down
Brown tinted eyes
Smiles that freeze time
Rings around the neck
A bust sculpted
In the coolness of dawn
Flawlessly enchanting
Since birth only the Shea oil
Has graced your body
It is only natural
The hair is jet black
Very TAMA natural grind
Fleeting dashes of your beauty on my mind
I remember!!
DejaVous!!!

On a windy sunny afternoon

I sit and ponder
In amazement and wonder
The root cause of the problem
But it is not them
I am the cause
Like a course
Of the river
Changing routes to overcome obstacles
I have spread my tentacles
Though I am human
What is man
That greed and avarice
Has become his Lot
Like a plot
It thickens, beyond understanding
If only we are standing
Can we see
Beyond the shallow green sea
Kola the nut
Though he is not a nut
Said it all.
It begins with you
Or should I say I?
Sorry.
Change is now. Within.
Until then……

Mr Accountability

Summoning all ye members of the forum.

All ye learned members come to this August setting where our tyrant would lay the way forward. Where are ye fair-minded men, among whom there are no equals?

Speak up! Speak up! For the patience of the citizens run thin. Yet they hide, hide behind one man of whom no one knows.

Who will speak for the masses? Where is that man of whom they speak, yet does not speak?

Speak Sir! Speak Sir!

For we are listening. Yes, the masses are listening. Yet he won't speak because no one knows his name.

Come! Come!

We summon you! The masses summon you. Where are you?

Who are you?

Why won't you come when we call?

Are you thus cruel that you respond not to those that summon you?

Awake for we are tired! We are bleeding! We are sick and hungry. Come! Please come!

Or we call you wrongly, without respect.

But forgive us for we are only human. Who can fault us, for as soon as we eat and drink, we become foolish?

Where are you MR? ACCOUNTABILITY? Where are YOU?

Ode to my Ghanaian love

She has closed
Forgotten all about us
I sit on the stoop
I crave a cry
She is too busy
Not to notice us
I persist till
Her soft melodic voice carries
"Hello Major"
I smile in wonder
Gaze. Into the (un)known
Pearly teeth cast unseen shadows
A sweet black neck becomes a pedestal
For a face sculpted by the Creator
I would give all to see all
Yet, I love what I see
An Afro Ghanaian beauty

Tears at 58

so much pain
I lean on a cane
I no longer walk
not to mention talk
not to mention a whisper
I just read the paper
we are 58
10 more years plus 48
20 more years plus 38
yet we are not straight
a country called Malaysia
on the continent of Asia
looked and laughed
the black star of Africa
the star with no luster
 the star with no shine
the black star
how then do we shine
public office is a vehicle to acquire wealth
to be ordinary is to have no good health
a very good network of bad roads
for us to hop along like toads
let there be light
but you have no right
nor do you have the sight
for there is no vision
as we have no mission
I have come to deliver
for I am only a messenger

The day after

God bless our homeland Ghana
There is no Manna
Only Hope
I am not on Dope
Integrity
Without Pity
Accountability
Minus Feeling Guilty
As a table is Set
So are our Mindset
Always begging for Alms
With outstretched Palms
A day After
I feel High
Together
No more Sigh
There is a new Wind
Coming from Behind
60 will be Better
59 will be Smiles
After so many Miles
No more Hindsight
We now have Foresight

...and I cannot sleep

...and I cannot sleep
Part of the reason why I cannot keep
My thoughts from roaming all over
A million thoughts to ponder
Domestic and international
Within the circuit of being a national
It shows in my writing
Pure hogwash; unable to combine two words
To make nonsense of my thoughts

..and still, I am awake
Thoughts lingering on a plane
Do make some noise lest I make
I would hate people to see me through the pane
It is not a window
It shows in my thinking
Jumbled thoughts, unable to follow a train
To make nonsense of my thinking

Now I will sleep
Hopefully, I will wake
I will have clearer thoughts
About the same issues
Turned uglier by the minute
In the jungle of it all
I crave nothing but two wishes
To sleep again
To be a baby again
These will but assure
With no definite measure

No care unlimited

Now I am assured I wrote utter nonsense!

Chapter 2 In the eye of the Lion

'Though many perceive him to be ruthless and full of anger, he is very patient. See him as he walks majestically. Try to catch a steady gaze into his eyes. There you find a sense of calmness. A sense of peace. A sense of patience. I have seen it all. I have looked into his eyes. He is a lion. Your grandfather'
That is how grandma described grandpa to me. We are sitting under one of the mango trees at the back of the house. It is the one near the wall. My aunt who is not my aunt is close and so is my dad. (I am imagining my grandma kissing my grandpa) I break out in laughter. I am not spared a stern look. "Do not be like your father. Look at him playing." I enjoy seeing my father as when he is young. Now I know he is not all that stern. I strayed off the path.Again. My grandma gets tired easily now. She is like a matriarch for the community. She serves as a counselor to the women of the town. My grandma runs the house. She does the cooking and cleaning with help from my aunts and uncles and sometimes their cousins.
My aunt who is not my aunt picks up the story.
She describes grandma's body when she was young. She runs inside to bring and show me the family album. As I thumb through the pages I scream and shout. My grandma is a curvaceous woman. After five kids, she still looked good for a lady of fifty-five. Wait! I see the look of doubt on your face. Come in. Stand right there. Yes that is my grandma. Now look at you. Close your mouth. Hahahhaha. Yes, she is that beautiful lady. In the doorway to your right is her husband. The very person my aunt who is not my aunt and I were just talking about. Do you mind sitting down as she tells us the story? I hope you don't mind sipping on some cool coconut juice or eating

tangerines? Have your pick of fruits. These are organic as you would say.

Aunt whose name I will not mention because she is no longer my aunt tells us of how grandma and grandpa met. She tells of the suitors that were arranged for grandma by her parents who were influential and wealthy folk of the town. Grandma rejected each of them. She tells of how grandma asked one suitor to bring her the eye of the lion just to scare him. At the mention of that incident, grandma springs up from her chair as though she has sensed her husband to be standing in the doorway to her left. "The lion, eye of the lion" she softly said. Grandpa smiled in acknowledgment. 'Mother of my heart' he boomed. 'Son' he called out to me 'do you know your grandma is me? She is my heartbeat. She is me.' I looked on as my uncles and household members came around. We all sat under the mango tree and talked. It is evening now and the sun has decided to go home and get some rest after along day.

Grandma tells of how grandpa did not budge in spite of all the suitors. Grandpa was seen as a bully and domineering, as a potential wife beater. This was because of his heavy build and constant frown on his face. Her parents would not allow them to be married. He refused to be daunted. 'Underneath all his strong man looks, he is a darling. Sweet at heart, very loving and patient. He told me the story of the patience of the lion. I accompanied him on one of his hunting trips and he pointed out to me the lion in his habitat. He showed me the patience in the lion's eyes as he waited to pounce. That day and ever since, I have always seen your grandpa as a lion.' Now you hear her own narrative of her husband. They have their moments, they say, but would never give each other up.

My story can only be told by me
My story is my experience
My story is I

My story is my story

I do not need your applause
I do not need your sympathy
I do not need your comfort
I speak from my heart
I hunt and fish in my mind
My story, our story, your story

Reflections out of memories

End of the year; time to reflect
I am not perfect
I strive to be who I want to be;
I am shaped by discipline;
A simple garment of principle
So as I sit to reflect, a hammer knocks my head
I refuse entry and it keeps knocking
Now my head hurts; the pain of memories
Cascading down the years like Niagara falls;
Bucket list. Hotel sleeps in the misty falls.
This month of intense reflection as it ushers in a new year;
The memory that I once had a mother;
She still smiles at me wherever I am
She caresses me through the wind
Touching me by rain or snow
I was birthed by a lovely sweet tall gigantic woman
5"2
December reminds me of the ensuing year
To write or not to write
To focus or lose out
To be in the service or do family matters;
Priorities
Schedules
Service to mankind
The beautiful thing I see is cutting down
Webs of hate encircling me
My tools of choice being love and persistence
Sharpened with focus, discipline, and principle
December memories: the words of my father
Guiding me as I walk the stony road; sometimes running and

falling
Guardian angels in physical and spirit-lifting me to continue
Face full of mud; bystanders laughing and wishing for that long
box;
My Father in Heaven who lives in me denying them that
laughing opportunity;
Determination and guidance,
Perseverance; all bracketed by a sense of purpose
Only aligning with like minds
Ready to catapult only onto the right pedestal
Conscience positioned on my neck
Refusing to bathe in the rivers of deceit
And clad me in a garment of lies,
No, I view the ensuing through a lens fashioned by my Creator
and polished by my hand
December memories need to dry out
Like clothing hung out to dry on a sunny wintry morning
Some hung me out to dry in the raw harmattan winds of Africa
Still, He who dwells in me...
Memories birthing goals that are attainable
In peace do I saunter
Towards my goals
Graceful and majestically like a horse"s canter.
Head high, eyes low, soft voice
Fade into the sunshine

Heaven

"Our Father, who art in Heaven..."
And when...
Psalm 23.
No log
Simply perfect
Yaaaaay!! Chant down Babylon
Oh no! What an error
No! Very right
Truth ...
Don't dare. Parables
You believe
Jesus (Spanish pronunciation) spoke.
Shortest verse.
I stand and dwell.
Peace

Cosmetics

We love to say all is well
Then again there is a word
Society claims to be concerned
Acting all cozy cozy
Conjugate: HYPOCRITE
New word: COSMETIC
Underneath; beneath
Burrowed into the soil
Growing tentacle-like roots
That is how the hate is in you
Then you come out in garments of filth
Golden with prejudice
Trimmed with pretense
Adorned in ornaments of spite, anger, bitterness, neglect,
depression.
Cosmetics that is what you have on.
It is okay to wipe off.
Let the world know who you are.
For now, we know you have on a lot of MAKEUP

Toddlers once

We love to say all is well
Then again there is a word
Society claims to be concerned
Acting all cozy cozy
Conjugate: HYPOCRITE
New word: COSMETIC
Underneath; beneath
Burrowed into the soil
Growing tentacle-like roots
That is how the hate is in you
Then you come out in garments of filth
Golden with prejudice
Trimmed with pretense
Adorned in ornaments of spite, anger, bitterness, neglect,
depression.
Cosmetics that is what you have on.
It is okay to wipe off.
Let the world know who you are.
For now, we know you have on a lot of MAKEUP

painting different colors

Round we go
encircling our minds
In catastrophic cacophony
Without recourse to
'Informed and qualitative
Yet even
Discerning
That which is a lie or truth
But then both be fact'
thinking!
Humpty dumpty they say
Was mended after he fell
again who has ever picked up
And put together a broken egg?
of only your mother were you born
Let not another think for you.
Think with them
In flowing rivers of wisdom

Changing minds

Swift she blows
On a very high low
Too humid this season
It is spring or rainy season
The wind
Very confusing.
Dry grass bringing forth
Green grass gasping for breath
Leaves born anew
Roots gnarled firmly askew
Earth static yet still wealthy
Man confused and not healthy.
That is the power of the mind
Unless we uproot that set
Setbacks will be the norm
That will be set
Forever
Need to change minds
Only for the better
Not for the matter
I am only a messenger.
I have come to deliver.

LOST

I lay here in somber reflection,
Not a moment of a feeling of affection;
It is total and utmost injection;
Into my heart and mind of rejection.
It is what I feel most;
I have run and lost;
I am wondering about the cost.
Water me with the frozen waters
Jolt me into a reality that matters
Will the sun rain its rays?
Will I be protected like the rose?
Will I seek refuge like a sunflower?
I will cast shadows
To give shade and joy.

The Funeral

We have come to mourn,
Many, like the teeth of corn,
We have been apart torn,
Coming here this morn.
In clothes never worn,
We have come to mourn.
In the colors of the rainbow,
Our culture is no more
Traditions are a bore
And longer at the core.
Rainbow is the new black,
Laughter to bid farewell.
I have come to mourn
Unlike you who choose
To seek one to moan
After a funeral celebration
For a life well-lived.
Though we cared not when you sought us
Yet to bid au revoir,
We are here.
Dirges are played
Few tears water the earth
Merriment for a new beginning
Footsteps pound the earth
Unto each his own
Unto each their story.
One day it said
We will meet again.

tOMMORROW

If I am here tomorrow,
I will be out of my borough.
There will be no need to burrow
Into a deep hole.
I am a human, not a mole.

If I am here tomorrow,
I will tread on the narrow.
Shaping my principles,
Forging into disciplines

Quick or slow to stop the damage,
To do so will stop the drainage.
Then closure; for it will be changed.

The dream

If I am here tomorrow,
I will be out of my borough.
There will be no need to burrow
Into a deep hole.
I am a human, not a mole.

If I am here tomorrow,
I will tread on the narrow.
Shaping my principles,
Forging into disciplines

Quick or slow to stop the damage,
To do so will stop the drainage.
Then closure; for it will be changed.

is this life?

.and it was in the cool of the night.
The sun had roasted the earth.
Many wished for the rain
But it was too warm for even a drizzle.
Even it was cumbersome to talk on the phone,
It was just chatting on different platforms.
Each claimed to love as brothers and sisters
Beautiful reading thoughts expressed
Nothing but stone wrapped in Candy wrapping
Finally, sleep crawled into the eyes
Souls given to the Creator to keep.
"I spoke to him last"
"he was my best friend"
"was he sick? How come we did not know?"
Too late.
No tears. No tears.
The crack of dawn brings light to the eyes.
It is the light of life.
What life?
Which life?

End of year

End of year
Reflections
Deflections
Erections
Elections
Selections
End of year
Laughter
Wailing
Smiling
Gnashing
Still a cycle
Break the mold
End of year
Fence; wall; division
View; top low
Still laughing
Total
Utter Nansins
My ribs. Better
End of year

My first Love

It was such heartbreak

Absolutely could not make

Any sense of our breakup, I

Was so heartbroken, could not in my life makeup, I

Struggled and watched you

As you paraded the corridors spreading your love.

I was devastated beyond comprehension,

Humility in gentility, understanding beyond the ordinary,

Kissing smoothly while caressing with a careless abandon

That drives the senses to heightened calm pitch

You took the first step of reconciliation,

You gave another chance when all stood against

You held me to your bosom and allowed me to breath in your sweet fragrance

I remember your first kiss; smooth, gentle, unwavering

You held me tight and I was in love

My dad was against our love, he preferred the other.

Mom loved you, no wonder you reached out when she lived to eternity

Glad we are together again.

My first love, Poetry.

A bridge to Verse 2

I have introduced you to my people as best as I can. Now I hope you understand when I refuse to align myself with these people. It is better for us to move forward as a people learning from our past than doing things on our own. You are right to admonish me for I was truly not there but then I was. I wish I could sleep for forever but if I do, you will never hear about my people nor know the truth. Our forebears have so much to teach us. Are we ready to learn?

We shall enjoy at the banquet before we take leave of my people. The spread being prepared is enough to feed the whole town for a week but we will feast for just a night. I am salivating so much. Look at my aunties and grandmother as they go about preparing. "Kwasi, stir the stewed beef. Kwasi taste the chicken soup. Kwasi is the rice done'? My secret has been revealed. Now you know how I got my culinary skills.

I feel out of place in my jeans and white polo shirt. Everyone is dressed in smocks/fugu for the men and kaba and sleet for the ladies. The dresses are colorful and the styles sewn protects the dignity and sanctity of the woman. Prints are made in Ghana with local symbols.

Libation is poured and grace is said. We are ready to eat. There is beef stew, chicken stew, fish stew, goat stew, stewed beans with boiled plantains, fried ripe plantains, yams, cooked white rice. There is also peanut butter soup, palm nut soup and light soup with fufu and rice balls. There is a whole roasted pig. My favorite. All too soon I have to leave. I want to enjoy my food. Eat all you can. No restrictions. Drink some palm wine. It is chilled. Just enjoy yourself. These are my people. You are home.

Let us cross the bridge

CPSIA information can be obtained
at www.ICGtesting.com
Printed in the USA
LVHW090428180720
661005LV00006B/838